Literacy
Activity Book

Year R Term 3

Louis Fidge

Letts
EDUCATIONAL

Acknowledgements
Extract from *Charles Tiger* by Siobhan Dodds, first published in the UK by Orchard Books in 1987, a division of The Watts Publishing Group Limited, 96 Leonard Street, London EC2A 4XD

Extract from *Goodnight Owl* by Pat Hutchins, published by Bodley Head. Used with permission of Random House UK Limited.

Here's a Little Mouse Hole from *Tickle My Nose and Other Action Rhymes* by Kaye Umansky (Puffin, 1999) Copyright © Kaye Umansky, 1999.

First published 2000

Letts Educational
9–15 Aldine Street, London W12 8AW
Tel: 020 8740 2270   Fax: 020 8740 2280

Text © Louis Fidge

Designed by Gecko Limited, Bicester, Oxon
Produced by Ken Vail Graphic Design, Cambridge

Colour reproduction by PDQ, Bungay, Suffolk

Illustrated by Graham-Cameron Illustration (Frank Endersby and Sue Woollatt), Simon Girling & Associates (Carol Daniel, Mimi Everett, Sue King and Mike Walsh), John Plumb, Sylvie Poggio Artists Agency (Bethan Matthews) and Maggie Sayer.

British Library Cataloguing-in-Publication Data
A CIP record for this book is available from the British Library

ISBN 1 84085 447 2

Printed in Spain by Mateu Cromo

Letts Educational, a division of Granada Learning Ltd. Part of the Granada Media Group.

Introduction

The Year R Literacy Textbooks:

- support the teaching of the Literacy Hour
- are best used along with the *YR Poster Packs* and *Teacher's Notes* which provide more detailed suggestions for development activities
- help meet the majority of the objectives of the National Literacy Strategy Framework (when used in conjunction with the *YR Poster Pack* and *Teacher's Notes*)
- are divided into three books, each containing one term's work
- contain ten units per term (equivalent to one unit a week)

- contain one Writing Focus unit each term to support compositional writing
- provide coverage of a wide range of writing, both fiction and non-fiction, as identified in the National Literacy Strategy Framework
- assume an adult (a teacher, parent or classroom assistant) will be supporting the children, reading to and with them, and mediating the tasks
- assume much of the work will be done orally, with written responses expected only as and when pupils have sufficient competence to record them.

Unit number →

Text for reading and discussion

Key teaching points

Text Level activities (purple)

Sentence Level activities (yellow)

Word Level activities (green)

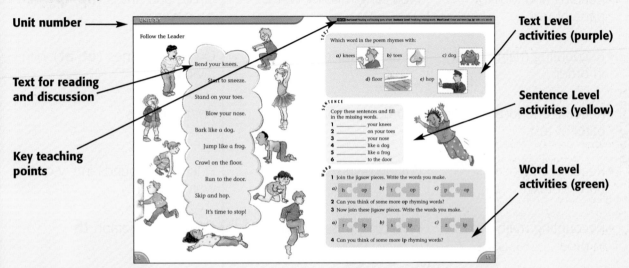

Writing Focus unit:

- appears on pages 26–29
- develops aspects of work covered in preceding ten units
- supports work on compositional writing
- contains support and suggestions for the teaching of essential writing skills
- assumes much work will be done orally through discussion
- assumes that an adult will act as a scribe, helping children record their ideas for much of the time, and that children will only be expected to record as their developing writing competencies allow.

Phonic Check-up:

- appears on pages 30–31
- reviews the phonic work covered in the preceding ten units
- may be used to provide a review of progress or as further practice in areas of concern.

High Frequency Word List:

- appears on page 32
- contains words that frequently appear in children's reading and writing
- may be used to help children to recognise these words on sight and spell them correctly
- provides an easily accessible resource for spelling and reading activities and a ready reference section.

	Focus	
Text Level	**Sentence Level**	**Word Level**
• Recounting main points in order	Predicting missing words	The alphabet
• Reading and locating parts of text	Checking sentences for sense	Building c-v-c words; medial vowels **o** and **e**
• Reading and locating parts of text	Predicting missing words	Rhyming
• Reading and locating parts of text	Reordering words	Building c-v-c words; medial vowels **a** and **e**
• Reading and locating parts of text	Predicting missing words	Onset and rimes (**op**, **ip**) with c-v-c words
• Recounting main points in order	Predicting missing words	Onset and rimes (**ut**, **at**) with c-v-c words
• Reading and locating parts of text	Reordering words	Animal noises
• Reading and locating parts of text	Writing own name	Final letter sounds in c-v-c words
• Recounting main points in order	Predicting missing words	Consonant digraph **th**
• Reading and locating parts of text	Checking sentences for sense	Rhyming; initial letters **g** and **m**
Writing Focus	*Writing a story; Writing instructions; Writing a rhyme; Writing captions; Writing a recount*	
Phonic Check-up	*Review of Word Level skills covered in Units 3.1–3.10*	

Year R, Term 3

CONTENTS

The Tiger Who Lost His Roar

*One morning Charles Tiger woke up without
his roar, so he went to look for it.*

Charles walked to the top of a
steep hill and found a bear –
but no roar.

He looked in the long grass and
found a snake – but no roar.

He looked in a deep river and
found a crocodile – but no roar.

He looked in the wet mud
and found an elephant – but
no roar.

He looked under a stone and
found a spider – and his great
big roar.

Charles Tiger was very
happy again.

Charles Tiger (slightly adapted) by Siobhan Dobbs

TEXT

Where did Charles look? Put these sentences in order.

◆ Charles looked in the long grass.

◆ Charles looked on the top of a steep hill.

◆ Charles looked in the wet mud.

◆ Charles looked under a stone.

◆ Charles looked in a deep river.

SENTENCE

Find the missing words.

1 Charles looked on the top of a _____ hill.

2 Charles looked in the _____ grass.

3 Charles looked in a _____ river.

4 Charles looked in the _____ mud.

WORD

1 Which letters are missing?

a b _ d e f _ h i _ k l _ n o _ q r s _ u v w _ y _

2 Which letters are missing?

A _ C D _ F G _ I J _ L M _

O P _ R _ T U _ W X _ Z

7

How to Make a Stick Puppet

You need:
- 2 paper plates
- a lollipop stick
- crayons
- wool
- glue

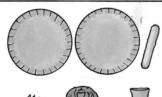

What you do:

Draw a happy face on one plate.

Draw a sad face on the other plate.

Glue the lollipop stick to the back of one plate.

Glue the two plates together.

Glue on the wool for hair.

TEXT

1 Make a list of things you need to make a stick puppet.

2 What is the first thing you do?

3 What is the last thing you do?

SENTENCE

Correct these sentences.

1 Draw a happy plate on one face.

2 Glue a sad face on the other plate.

3 Draw the lollipop stick to the back of one plate.

4 Glue the three plates together.

WORD

1 Which words can you make from these word sums?

h + o + p

m + o + p

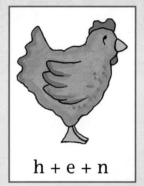

h + e + n

p + e + n

2 What is missing – **o** or **e**?

p_n

h_n

h_p

m_p

9

Cat and Mouse

Hickory, dickory, dock.
The mouse ran up the clock;
The clock struck one,
The mouse ran down,
Hickory, dickory, dock.

Pussy cat, Pussy cat, where have you been?
I've been up to London to look at the Queen.
Pussy cat, Pussy cat, what did you there?
I frightened a little mouse under her chair.

TEXT

1 What ran up the clock?

2 What time was it?

3 Why did the cat go to London?

4 What did the cat do in London?

SENTENCE

Find the missing words.

1 The mouse _____ up the clock.

2 The clock _____ one.

3 I _____ a little mouse under her chair.

WORD

1 Match up the pairs of rhyming words.

sock

sick

suck

chick

duck

lock

2 Think of some words that rhyme with:

sack

peck

When I Grow Up

TEXT

1 Which of these things does the boy want to be?

a) an astronaut

b) a footballer

c) a sailor

d) a dancer

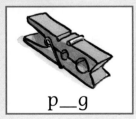

e) a doctor

f) a mechanic

2 What do you want to be when you grow up?

SENTENCE

Put the words in order.

1 want I be to astronaut an
2 want I be to mechanic a
3 want I be to dancer a
4 want I be to workman a
5 want I be to sailor a

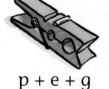

WORD

1 Which words can you make from these word sums?

m + a + n

v + a + n

l + e + g

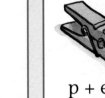

p + e + g

2 What is missing – **a** or **e**?

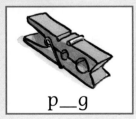

p_g

m__n

v__n

l_g

13

Follow the Leader

Bend your knees.

Start to sneeze.

Stand on your toes.

Blow your nose.

Bark like a dog.

Jump like a frog.

Crawl on the floor.

Run to the door.

Skip and hop.

It's time to stop!

TEXT

Which word in the poem rhymes with:

a) knees  *b)* toes *c)* dog

d) floor  *e)* hop

SENTENCE

Copy these sentences and fill in the missing words.

1 _____ your knees
2 _____ on your toes
3 _____ your nose
4 _____ like a dog
5 _____ like a frog
6 _____ to the door

WORD

1 Join the jigsaw pieces. Write the words you make.

a) h op   *b)* t op   *c)* p op

2 Can you think of some more **op** rhyming words?

3 Now join these jigsaw pieces. Write the words you make.

a) r ip   *b)* s ip   *c)* z ip

4 Can you think of some more **ip** rhyming words?

15

The Hairdresser

I went to have my hair cut.

I sat on a big chair.

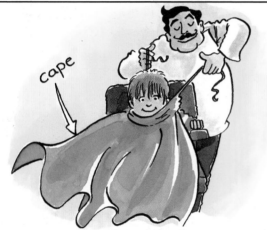

The hairdresser put a cape on me.

The hairdresser combed my hair.

The hairdresser cut my hair.

Some hair went down my neck.
It tickled.

TEXT

Put these sentences in order.

◆ The hairdresser combed my hair.

◆ I sat on a big chair.

◆ I went to have my hair cut.

◆ The hairdresser cut my hair.

◆ The hairdresser put a cape on me.

SENTENCE

Choose the best word for each gap.

1 You _____ (sit/look) in a mirror.

2 You _____ (brush/sit) on a chair.

3 You _____ (sit/cut) with scissors.

4 You _____ (brush/look) your hair.

WORD

1 List some things you can find in a hairdresser's shop.

2 Join these jigsaw pieces. Write the words you make.

a) c ut   *b)* n ut   *c)* h ut

3 Can you think of some more **ut** rhyming words?

4 Now join these jigsaw pieces. Write the words you make.

a) c at   *b)* r at   *c)* b at

5 Can you think of some more **at** rhyming words?

Goodnight Owl

Owl tried to sleep.

The bees buzzed, buzz, buzz,
and Owl tried to sleep.

The squirrels cracked nuts, crunch, crunch,
and Owl tried to sleep.

The crows croaked, caw, caw,
and Owl tried to sleep.

The woodpecker pecked, rat-a-tat! rat-a-tat!
and Owl tried to sleep.

The starlings chittered, twit-twit, twit-twit,
and Owl tried to sleep.

The jays screamed, ark, ark,
and Owl tried to sleep.

The cuckoos called, cuckoo, cuckoo,
and Owl tried to sleep.

The doves cooed, croo, croo,
and Owl tried to sleep.

Then darkness fell and the moon came up.

And there wasn't a sound.

Owl screeched, screech, screech, and woke
everyone up.

Goodnight Owl by Pat Hutchins

TEXT

Match the names to the correct pictures.

| bee | squirrel | crow | woodpecker | dove | owl |

SENTENCE

Put these words in order.

1 bees the buzzed

2 squirrels the nuts cracked

3 crows the croaked

4 woodpecker the pecked

5 doves the cooed

6 owl sleep to tried

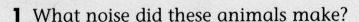

WORD

1 What noise did these animals make?

a) the bees   **b)** the squirrels   **c)** the crows

d) the woodpeckers   **e)** the starlings   **f)** the jays

g) the cuckoos   **h)** the doves   **i)** the owl

2 Name some of the noises that other animals make.

Here's a Little Mouse Hole

Try these actions.

Here's a little mouse hole,
Mousy's peeping out.
She looks to the left, she looks to the right –
Is anyone about?

She tiptoes to the pantry,
She nibbles at the cheese,
She nibbles at the flour bag,
And she gives a great big sneeze. **ATCHOO!**

Here lies a kitty cat
Dozing in the sun.
Look, he's pricked his ears up!
Run, mouse, run!

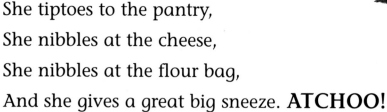

Back into the mouse hole,
Safe as safe can be,
Naughty little mouse says,
"YOU CAN'T CATCH ME!"

By Kaye Umansky from Tickle My Nose

TEXT

Who did each thing – the cat or the mouse?

1 Who lived in a hole?

2 Who likes cheese?

3 Who sneezed?

4 Who was asleep in the sun?

5 Who said, "You can't catch me!"?

SENTENCE

1 Write your name.

2 Think of a good name for the mouse.

3 Now think of a good name for the cat.

WORD

1 Choose a letter from the box. Finish each word.

ru__   ru__   ru__

2 Choose a letter from the box. Finish each word.

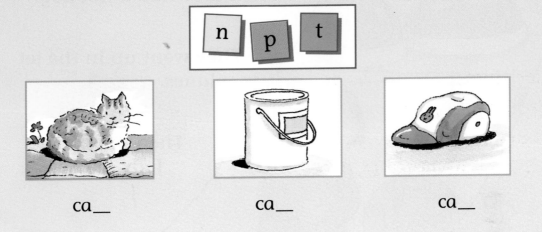

ca__   ca__   ca__

21

Up and Down and Round About

Jake and Jody went to the funfair.

They went round and round on a roundabout.

Then they had a toffee apple.

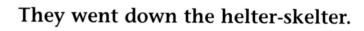

They went down the helter-skelter.

Then they had an ice cream.

They went in and out on the dodgem cars.

Then they had a hot dog.

They went up in the jet planes.

Then Jake and Jody felt ill!

TEXT

Put these sentences in order.

◆ Jake and Jody went down the helter-skelter.

◆ Jake and Jody went on a roundabout.

◆ Jake and Jody went in the jet planes.

◆ Jake and Jody went on the dodgem cars.

SENTENCE

Copy and fill in the missing words.

1 Jake and Jody went _____ the funfair.

2 They went _____ and _____ on a roundabout.

3 They went _____ the helter-skelter.

4 They went _____ and _____ on the dodgem cars.

5 They went _____ in the jet planes.

WORD

1 Add **th** to make some words.

__ick

__in

__ink

ba__

pa__

mo__

2 Which other words do you know that have **th** in?

23

The Sun is Hot

The sun is hot.

An ice cream is cold.

A baby is young.

A grandfather is old.

A car goes fast.

A snail goes slow.

A red light means 'stop'.

A green light means 'go'.

At night it's dark.

In the morning it's light.

The sun says, "Good morning".

And the moon says, "Good night".

Morning!

Night!

TEXT

1 What is hot?

2 What is cold?

3 Who is young?

4 Who is old?

5 What goes fast?

6 What goes slow?

7 What means 'stop'?

8 What means 'go'?

SENTENCE

Correct these sentences.

1 An ice cream is hot.

2 A baby is old.

3 A snail goes fast.

4 A green light means 'stop'.

5 At night it is light.

6 The sun comes out at night.

WORD

1 Name some things that go fast and slow.

2 Match up the pairs of rhyming words.

bat			wig
hen			mat
dig			bud
hot			pen
mud			cot

1. Writing a story

My name is Leo the Lion.
I have lost my roar.
Make up a story about how
I find it again.

Leo looked in a bush.
He found a _____
– but no roar.

Leo looked in a tree.
He found a _____
– but no roar.

Leo looked in a river.
He found a _____
– but no roar.

Leo looked in the _____ .
He found a _____
– and he found his roar.

ROARRRRR!

2. Writing instructions

How to make a mask

What you need:

Find the things you need.

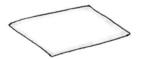

| piece of cardboard | scissors | crayons | string | wool | glue stick |

What you do:

Write some instructions for what you have to do.

3. Writing a rhyme

Fill in the missing words.

Put up your hand.   Play in a _____.

Touch your ear.   Shake with _____.

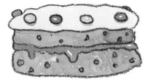

Hiss like a snake.   Bake a _____.

Drink some tea.   Swim in the _____.

Sit in that _____!   Go to the fair.

4. Writing captions

When I grow up I want to be an astronaut.

What do you want to be when you grow up?

Draw some pictures.

Write a sentence under each picture.

5. Writing a recount

I went to the hairdresser. Write about a visit you have made to the doctor or to the dentist.

Plan your story.

◆ Who did you go with?

◆ Why did you go?

◆ What did you do?

◆ What did you see?

◆ What happened?

Draw some pictures.

Make up a sentence about each picture.

Phonic Check-up

1 Write the letters in alphabetical order.

2 Make the words. Match them to the pictures.

c + o + t   m + u + g   p + o + t   j + u + g

3 Put in the missing **u**. Read the words you make.

d__ck   l__ck   s__ck   t__ck

4 Join the jigsaw pieces. Read the words you can make.

l   eg   p   eg   b   eg

c   ap   m   ap   t   ap

5 Choose one of the missing letters to finish these words.

b — g	n — p	t — g	p — n
			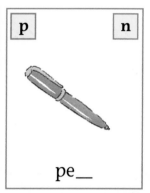
ba__	cu__	ha__	pe__

6 Put in the missing **th**. Read the words you make.

__in	__ick	ba__	mo__

7 Match up the pairs of words that rhyme.

bag 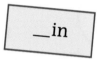　　　　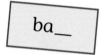 wet

net 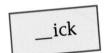　　　　 mix

six 　　　　 wag

fox 　　　　 jug

mug 　　　　 box

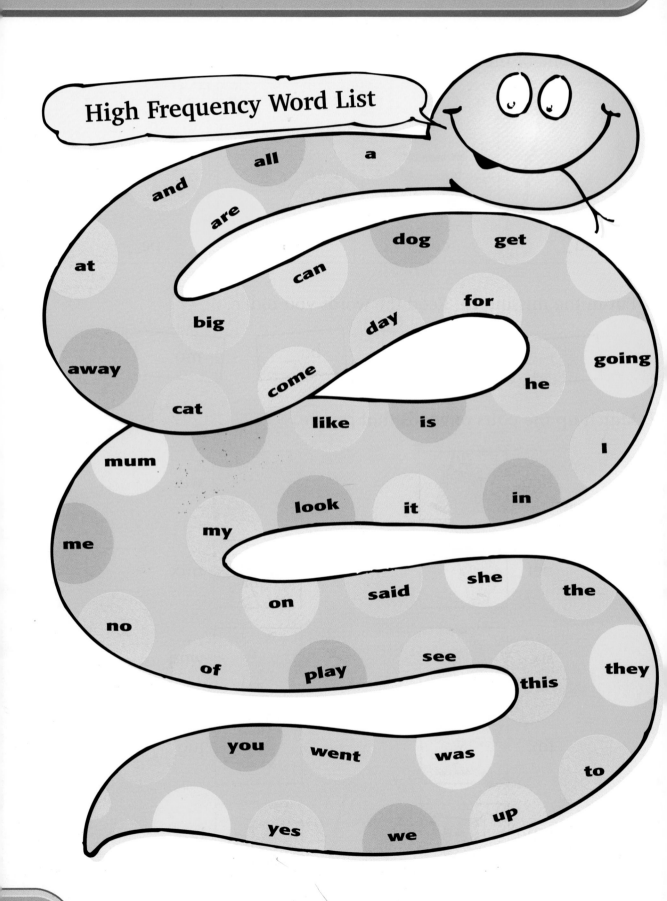

High Frequency Word List

a
all
and
are
at
can
dog
get
big
for
day
away
going
come
he
cat
like
is
mum
I
look
it
in
my
me
she
the
on
said
no
see
they
of
play
this
you
went
was
to
yes
we
up